LIFE IN REGENCY

CW00659760

Front Cover illustration: The Mail Coach leaving Beverley by the North Bar.

Life in
REGENCY
BEVERLEY

Prudence Bebb

William Sessions Limited
York, England

ISBN 1 85072 303 6

In memory of my dear friend
Jenny Gouch

Acknowledgements

THE AUTHOR WISHES TO EXPRESS her appreciation to the staff at York City Library and those at the East Riding Archives. She is grateful to Mr and Mrs J. Booth for allowing her to look round their Georgian home. She thanks Jill Moger, the sculptor, for depicting Joseph Coltman's hobby-horse.

Printed in 11 on 12 point Bembo Typeface
by Sessions of York
The Ebor Press
York YO31 9HS, England

Contents

List of Illustrations

The Prince Regent.

I
1811

JANE AUSTEN WAS CORRECTING the publisher's proofs of *Sense and Sensibility* in 1811. She wrote to her sister: "I am never too busy to think of S and S. I can no more forget it than a mother can forget her sucking child."

Napoleon was ruling conquered nations, yet a would-be poet in Britain wrote:

> "But Wellington, 'tis hoped will soon
> Drive the fell tyrant from his Throne;
> Destroy his army, foot and horse,
> Tho' charging with inferior force..."

Probably the booted British army would have liked the Real Japan Blacking currently being sold by Mr James the Perfumer in Beverley because "This invaluable composition, with half the usual labour, produces the most brilliant jet-black ever beheld, affords peculiar nourishment to the leather... and will retain its virtues in any climate..."

Despite world-stirring events, gentlemen in Beverley were more concerned to know if Mr Bethell's bay colt, loyally called Wellington, would win the Gold Cup on the Westwood.

A royal gentleman, who also appreciated a good horse, had just succeeded to his father's responsibilities. He was George, Prince of Wales and eldest son of old King George III.

Not that the Prince had become king, not yet. His father was too ill to do the job any longer. Suffering from porphyria, he was too mentally deluded to sign an Act of Parliament and so the Prince had been given the title of Prince Regent with the tasks that fell to the sovereign but not his title.

It would be another nine years before the Prince Regent became King George IV. Those years are called the Regency and in this little book we discover what the people of Beverley were doing during that time.

Royal Mail Coach from a painting by Herring.

The Beverley Mail

SCARLET WHEELS SPUN ALONG the turnpike road taking the mail coach from York to Beverley. Just before Grimston, the guard stood up on the boot and blew his horn. This alerted the pike-keeper so when the red and black coach reached Grimston Bar the toll-gate was standing open and they rolled through without slowing down.

Then over Kexby Bridge, crossing the River Derwent into the East Riding, through Wilberfoss passing the *Anchor Inn*, past the bow-windowed inn at Barmby Moor, the coach rattled and rumbled faster than the stage could go. It carried less passengers; there might be one on the box seat beside the driver but not more than three were allowed on the roof and they were forbidden to distract the guard from his responsibilities. It was his job to get the mails (locked in the box under his feet) safely to Beverley, stopping *en route* at Market Weighton and Pocklington to leave their bags of letters.

The horses strained in their collars climbing the steep hill onto the Wolds. They skirted the pond at Bishop's Burton, as it was then called. As they approached Killingwold Grave, the guard blew his horn again to ensure that the toll-gate would be opened.

Mail coaches often ran through thick mist which filled the lungs, hailstones that rattled on the roof, east winds that made one's eyes water and rain that stung the cheeks. A guard needed to be tough. Fortunately Mr Turner, Beverley's chemist, sold Church's Cough Drops, which had worked wonders for Thomas Edmunds, guard of the Birmingham and Sheffield Mail. He declared that "His life was preserved to his wife and family by the sole use of Church's Cough Drops." A bottle, bought in Sheffield High Street, gave him instant relief "when he had not the expectation of living many minutes, with his wife and children crying round him." This lachrymose scene was not repeated as he swallowed five bottles of the remedy and was able to don his red coat and take up his perch on the Sheffield Mail again.

It was late in the day when the Beverley Mail topped the rise but in summer weather the roof passengers could see the towers of the Minster.

The coach crossed the Westwood where five windmills pierced the skyline. As it reached the crossroads, almost all of Beverley was on the right. On the left a broad country lane was bordered by some handsome houses belonging to Beverley's more affluent folk and including the elegant town house of the Sykes family whose country home was, and still is, Sledmere.

The driver on the box adjusted his reins, making a loop in the off lead rein and another in the rein governing the near wheeler. The four horses turned and took the coach under the Tudor archway. The three passengers on the roof probably removed their tall-crowned hats from an instinctive fear that they would hit the roof. (If Tony Weller had been there no doubt he would have warned them not to lose their heads.)

They went through the shadowy bar, passing Amphion House on their left, and emerged into the wide street. On the right was the terrace of brick houses which is still there. The mail rumbled past the beautiful St Mary's Church on the left. The busy coaching inn, called the *Tiger*, was opposite on the right. The *Tiger* is still there but has become a row of shops. Beyond it, the *Beverley Arms* was a hostelry which some people still called by its old name, *The Blue Bell*.

The guard's responsibility was not over yet. The letters had to be taken to the Post Office in Toll Gavel. They were expected because everyone knew that the mail coach was very rarely late.

There the bag of mail would be sorted. The letters came folded, addressed on the front and sealed on the back. The usual seal was a gummed wafer, which was a small circle holding the top fold to the rest. An important document or a letter from a Very Important Person would have a waxed seal impressed with the device engraved on the sender's ring.

There was not a single letter with a stamp on it; they had not been invented. The recipient had to pay for the letter which was all very well if it was wanted but to pay for a letter, which you would rather not receive, was most annoying. It could be quite expensive even if you did want it. However, you were given a choice – pay for it or leave it but you couldn't read it before deciding.

It was unfortunate if Aunt Lizzie had written one of her long rigmaroles because the longer the letter the more you had to pay; its cost was determined by the number of pages. Of course, Aunt Lizzie might

The old Tiger Inn.

*Amphion House
beside North Bar.*

be one of the clever people who "crossed their lines". This meant that when they had covered a page with closely written words, they turned it at right angles and wrote over their previous lines. You needed to be even cleverer than the writer to decipher the letter and you required exceptional eyesight too. However, if Aunt Lizzie made a habit of crossing her lines, you began to acquire a facility for reading them, whether they were worth the effort or not. After all, she had tried to save you money.

There were other ways of doing that. The artful correspondent was not defeated by the Post Office rules.

Some folk invented their own code. "If I write Mr Arthur Smith, it means I cannot come. If I've put Arthur Smith, Esq., I shall be in Beverley on Saturday." Or it might simply be: "A couple of full stops after your name means Yes. If I've only put a comma, the answer is No." Then the addressee went to the Receiving Office and asked, "Are there any letters for me?". Upon being shown one with the coded address, he only had to say that he did not want it. Then there was nothing to pay but he had learnt what he wanted to know.

Some of the letters in the mail bag were not for Beverley people but they came by the same route. Correspondence for Bridlington, Driffield, Scarborough and Whitby was sent on its way by Mr Gardham who was in charge of the Beverley Post Office.

Mail Guard.

To Beverley by Stages

ANYONE IN LONDON WHO wanted to visit Scarborough, could catch the stage-coach which went along the eastern route through Stilton, Peterborough, Lincoln, Hull and Beverley. When the coach stopped at the *Bell Inn*, Stilton, they were fortified with some of the landlady's famous cheese but they were weary by the time they reached Barton.

At this point they met a big obstacle. In front of them was the silver-grey Humber, broad and tidal and smelling of the sea. Ocean-going ships sailed along this river and there was no bridge to span the wide expanse which washed the low banks. This was where junior travellers experienced excitement for the only way to cross to Hull and Beverley was by the ferry.

Stage-coach.

Passengers from York would be very weary by the time they reached the welcome of the *Beverley Arms*. In winter they would be relieved to see it or the *Tiger Inn* after a cold journey when flurrying snowflakes whitened the coachman's shoulders and settled on the horses' manes.

The *White Horse* in Hengate was another stopping place for coaches. In recent times it has been called Nellie's but now has its original name restored.

When Beverlonians wanted to travel to other parts of the country, they usually went first to Leeds where they could change coaches to go to Manchester, Liverpool, Chester and farther west to Holyhead. People wishing to make these journeys began at the *Cross Keys*, an inn run by Mr Simpson, where they could reserve a place on the stage-coach or even arrange to send a parcel on it. Their name and destination would be written in a book with the date when they wanted to travel. So they had "booked" their seat and would have to arrive by eight on the morning of their departure.

There they encountered a bustling scene. The guard took charge of their parcels and expected a generous tip in return. If they had only paid for an outside seat, he would produce the ladder so they could climb to the roof. In summer it was a good position, so elevated that you could see over the hedges and even into the upstairs windows of cottages on the route. In winter it was terribly exposed to wind-chill or soaking rain. If the weather was foggy, you coughed and inhaled the dank air. A seat inside was twice as expensive and warmer but it was very confined. Someone's elbow might be stuck in your ribs and you might long for fresh air if your companions seldom bathed or if they carried odorous provisions such as fish, cheese and game.

For a while, after Nelson's most famous battle, the coach which left Mr Simpson's inn for York and Leeds was called *Trafalgar*. By the Regency its name had been altered but was still patriotic; it was called the *True Briton*. It took seventeen hours from the start in Hull until it reached the *Golden Lion* in Manchester. In York it stopped at the *White Swan* in Pavement and that is where York people embarked if they were going to Beverley.

Young lady in a spencer which was a short jacket.

I V

Shutters and Shoescrapers

IN THE DUSK OF A winter evening flickering firelight cast shadows on timbered ceilings and lamplight shone through fanlights. Many of Beverley's homes were old cottages with a modern frontage. The visitor would rap the urn-shaped door-knocker (or the ring held in a lion's mouth) on a six-panelled Georgian door but when he was admitted, he found himself in a low, stone-flagged hallway. If he was tall, he might even need to bow his head to avoid the lintel of an interior door for this house, which at first appeared to be built in the reign of good King George, was in fact much older. It had been made to look fashionable with a new façade of bricks and probably a roof of pantiles. However, if you went into the yard behind it, you might discover that the back of the roof was still covered with slates. It was cheaper not to cover the whole roof with pantiles and most guests would never see the back of the old house. They would be entertained in the front rooms whilst the servants worked in the original Tudor portion.

More affluent householders purchased old cottages for demolition and then built a smart house on the site. This new home was designed by a local craftsman who had studied the plans of fashionable architects. He could gratify his employer's vanity with the latest style in pillars to flank the front door and include elegant alcoves on either side of the drawing-room fireplace where pretty china or leather-bound books could be displayed.

Some of the middle-aged and elderly Beverlonians were living in houses bought in their youth or inherited from Grandpapa whose portrait in a gilded frame hung above the best fireplace. Many of these houses had been built by William Middleton who sold them early in the reign of George III. Some of them remain and we can admire those at 74 and 76 Lairgate.

Walking beside the terrace which stands just inside the North Bar, it is easy to imagine the Regency people who entered these houses. The

Georgian frontages with narrow bricks and sash windows.

In Highgate.

Lairgate.

Regency shoppers were accustomed to bow windows.

The bottom left hand window is a Yorkshire Light.

Doorcase with plaster decoration.

Rails and shoe scraper in Combe Lane.

13

young lady in bonnet and spencer walking across Beverley's cobbles could feel them through her pumps and was in danger of twisting her ankle; but when she reached the row of elegant houses by the Bar, she could hold the iron hand rail as she mounted the steps. Gentlemen, in dark blue tail coats with brass buttons, discussed the merits of horses which would run the next day and reached the terrace with mud on their boots. No matter: it could be scraped off on the iron boot-scraper attached to the hand rail.

As darkness came some people pulled the shutters across the inside of their windows for protection. If the window was in a deep embrasure, the shutters folded back in daylight and fitted neatly into the wall.

Not all householders felt the need for shutters. There are many houses in Highgate which never had them so obviously it was considered a safe street.

Like the eyes in a face, it is the sash windows which give character to so many façades in Beverley. They vary in size; the bigger ones are drawing room windows and the smallest ones are on the top floor which is often the third storey. But all are made of small panes because no one

Plastered ceiling in the present Lairgate Hotel.

Cantilever staircase in Lairgate.

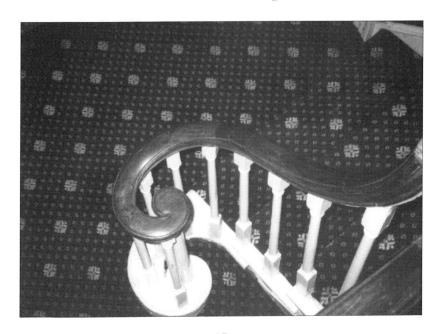

Step rails, North Bar Within.

could make sheet glass. Glass was blown, often leaving the mark of the pipe in a thickened centre. The little oblong panes were held in glazing bars to make a bigger window. During the Regency the windows looked lighter because their glazing bars were slender whereas the houses built in Grandpapa's day had thicker glazing bars.

All the affluent owners of sash windows could open and shut them safely as they were held by a sash cord running through a groove in the wooden framework. It wasn't so easy for the inhabitants of humbler homes whose tiny windows had no sash cord. If the owner opened one and leant out to call to a friend, he had to hold the window open with his hand. If he was so involved in a conversation that he forgot to keep his hand in position, the window dropped onto his neck, probably reminding him of what had happened recently to so many French people. No wonder some folk hammered a nail into the wood and rested the window on that.

Perhaps those cottagers, who had retained their Yorkshire Lights, were wise. These little windows slid horizontally and you could stick your head safely out of those that were not too small.

Not that Regency people were for ever opening windows. On the contrary, many of them thought that the air was "pernicious" and that it was wiser not to let too much of it into the room. Anyway Beverlonians would get more than a whiff of sickly odour from the tanneries if they did open windows.

Any fortunate gentleman who could pay for marble might adorn his house with a fashionable fireplace. He would probably employ Mr Appleton Benison, a builder and marble mason who had done work in Hull and had premises in Lairgate. Mr Benison built Beverley's gaol and lost money at that job because the price of timber rose so much during the Regency that the sum originally agreed for his remuneration was quite inadequate. The committee, who had originally agreed to pay eight and a half thousand, decided to add a furthur thousand pounds because Mr Benison had lost so much on the deal.

The present Lairgate Hotel gives a good idea of the type of house owned by Beverley's well-to-do inhabitants. This three-storeyed house has a fine entrance hall with a cantilever staircase.

V

Flying Colours

WELLINGTON COULD RUN VERY fast and had good staying power, (an excellent quality in a general) so had his half-brother. But Wellington was not a duke; he was a horse – a bay colt, to be precise, belonging to Mr Richard Bethell, one of Beverley's Justices of the Peace. Wellington's half-brother was another bay colt, son of the same father, Beningbrough, who was a well-known racehorse.

Mr Bethell would be able to watch his horse from the stand where local gentlemen gathered in the Long Room before each race meeting on the Westwood. Mr Bethell would have purchased a round silver ticket which made him eligible to watch the races from an elevated position, although not all the others there held silver tickets because no one checked them and some men borrowed tickets or even dared to enter without one at all. The stand was over fifty years old and was intended to give patrons a good view; it also kept them from rubbing shoulders with the *hoi polloi*. Races were meant for the enjoyment of gentlemen but the local inhabitants jostled on the Westwood. Critical persons complained that they did not add to the tranquility of the verdant scene "though they certainly do to the noise and hubbub".

In Regency days a race usually had only two or three participants; their owners and their friends bet on the results and settled up their bets in gentlemanly fashion at one of the inns after the races were over. There were no bookies and no one expected a farm labourer, cobbler or chapman to make a wager with a landowner. However, if the local crowd wanted to lay odds on a winner, they made for the "betting post", which stood like a signpost set into the grass.

Wellington, running for the Gold Cup at Beverley in June 1811, had some formidable opposition which included the winner of the cup at Catterick although that horse was deliberately handicapped with three pounds extra weight to carry. Mr Treacher's bay filly was the daughter of

Two racehorses.

Delpini, a well-known horse of good bloodstock which had sired some other promising racers.

The same day they ran two-mile heats designed for three and four year-olds, contending for a fifty pound plate. Heats usually lasted for two miles and it was not unusual for young men on horseback to follow the contenders trying to keep up with them. At the end the horses would be extremely hot so they were rubbed down with wooden swipers to remove the sweat.

The cups and salvers awarded at the races were paid for by subscriptions and the local innkeepers were expected to give generously towards them because the race brought them trade. Not only did visitors spend a few nights at the inns but the horses were stabled there too. No horse-boxes cluttered the roads. In days before mechanical transport, competing horses might have come to Beverley on their own hooves even from so far away as Newmarket. Punters, studying form, had to remember that a horse of excellent breeding might nevertheless be hampered by tiredness. This was taken into consideration when wagers were laid. Some gentlemen were not above subterfuge and brought their horses to Beverley a few days before expected; then a local innkeeper would be induced to keep the horse hidden until shortly before its race so that it was rested when everyone thought it would be weary. Usually Beverley Races were held the week after York's Spring Meeting so most entries would come about thirty miles.

Friday 14th June was the day when horses of all ages might race together; the weights they were to carry varied according to the horse's age. To preserve equality of opportunity, horses which had already run a race that season were to be handicapped by 3lbs and any which had won two races had a five pound handicap. Beverley town had raised £50 as a prize for one of the races. Supposing only one horse turned up, what then? It was automatically awarded £20 and its entrance fee of two guineas was returned.

That day gave spectators an opportunity to see another of Beningbrough's offspring running. Its mother was Roseberry and it belonged to Mr R C Burton.

Gentlemen in the Beverley neighbourhood were fortunate to live in the county from which most of England's best racehorses came. Some fine stallions with Arab blood in them were at stud here. Yorkshire mares were mated with them and some very fast offspring were produced. Beningbrough himself was living at Masham where there was spare accommodation for mares and their grooms. An East Riding gentleman could send a mare up to Masham and for five guineas she could be mated with a splendid blood horse. The Bethell and Strickland families bred superb racing horses.

1811 was a good season for breeding; the grass in Yorkshire was succulent and Beningbrough was in the best of health. Then there was Young Woodpecker, a fine steed, living near Jervaulx Abbey and available for mating there. He was a very well-known horse so it would be well worth the trouble of sending a mare to him.

One reason for holding the races was to encourage the breeding of good bloodstock but another reason was pleasure. Beverley Races brought fashionable gentlemen and their ladies to the town. Sir Mark Sykes was a keen supporter of "The Turf" (as racing was called) and had his town house in Beverley where he and his guests could stay during Race Week. So popular was racing that even some peers of the realm came to Beverley's course. It was a time of jollification, attractive to the gentry and lucrative to the town. There would be assemblies held where a young girl from Beverley might find herself hand-in-hand with a viscount as she danced her way down a set where partners were continually changing.

Gentlemen in dark blue coats with brass buttons and high neckcloths discussed "horseflesh" over a wine glass. Anxious and excited voices commented on "the going". The rain had died, the ground was no longer squelchy and which horses would it suit best? There were not so many possibilities as there are today seeing that the field was much smaller. It was their ancestry that caused most comment. Who was the sire? and who was the dam?

Sometimes the gentlemen themselves rode their own horses in the race. In 1812 such a race was open to horses of all ages but certificates had to be produced from the breeders.

Some gentlemen, rather in the manner of a sweepstake, subscribed the money themselves to pay for the trophy. In 1812 Mr Bethell, Mr Thomas Duncombe and Sir Mark Sykes each put in twenty guineas and advertised for seven more gentlemen to do the same. With the hundred guineas they would buy a gold plate and the subscribers would all enter horses for the race which was to be four miles long and horses of all ages might be admitted but handicaps of weight would be used to give all a chance.

Not everyone wanted a place on the stand; more than one man would prefer to drive to the Westwood in a fashionable curricle (a two-wheeled open carriage pulled by a pair of horses) with a pretty young woman sitting up beside him. The curricle could be parked in a suitable position and the pair could watch the races from it. No doubt the two horses, harnessed one either side of the pole, watched too; intelligent ears pricked up as hooves pounded the green earth so fast that no one could see the exact movement of the legs and there were no cameras to record them. Artists painted their impressions depicting the legs flat out, fore and aft, because they had never seen the rounded motion which photographs show to us. As hooves thudded, the sun cast shadows of favourite fillies over the grass but a neck-and-neck result might be hard to determine; there was no photo-finish although there were ribbons across the track at the end to help in seeing which horse arrived first at the finish.

Gentlemen, who wished to enter horses for the races had to send their names by January 1st to the clerk of the course, Mr Skelton, although the races themselves might be in June but there was much organising to be done beforehand.

On way to races.

Some owners would be hopefully visiting the blood-stock stables to which they had sent their mares. In 1812 they only needed to send their mares to Bishop Burton where the famous Cerberus was at stud. If you sent a horse to be mated with Cerberus, it cost you five guineas plus a furthur ten shillings and sixpence for your groom's board and lodging. It was too good an opportunity to miss because Cerberus was the grandson of Marske. Every racing gentleman knew what that meant. Marske was a well-bred Yorkshire horse who had been sent to Windsor where he sired Eclipse and Eclipse was the greatest racehorse ever.

Trafalgar was at stud at Leconfield Park so, while his mare was awaiting the services of Trafalgar, a Beverley gentleman could ride three miles through the lanes to Leconfield to see how she was getting on.

The names of horses could often tell the initiated where they or their parents had been bred. Sir B Graham's grey horse was named Sledmere, Mr Duncombe's bay filly was sired by Hambletonian and many racehorses were trained on the Hambleton Hills above the Vale of York. Sir Mark Masterman Sykes of Sledmere and Mr Duncombe were the stewards and had to settle any disputes which arose during the race meeting.

On George III's birthday (4th June) the Gold Cup attracted ten subscribers but the stewards' own horses came in 4th and 5th. The cup was won by Mr Burton's brown colt, Don Julian. The next day Mr Duncombe had the consolation of seeing his chestnut mare, Laurel Leaf, come second in a four-mile sweepstake which the *York Herald* later described as: "A very severe and well-contested race and won with difficulty," which was a great credit to Laurel Leaf because the winner, Mr Uppleby's bay filly Harriett, was very good bloodstock. Anyway, the same day the three-mile heats attracted a big crowd of spectators. Don Julian was running again and betting stakes changed when people saw him in the heats. Finally he won in a canter which would not surprise those who knew that his father was Stamford who was at stud at Cantley near Doncaster. Those, who wished to leave a mare to be served by him, had to pay £10 and 10/6d for the groom. This was twice as much as most stud charges. Yet it was understandable because Stamford was the grandson of Eclipse – that great horse whose name is remembered today and who is the ancestor of so many superlative horses.

Beverley was a very lively place during race week. All tastes were catered for; the inns served more people at each Ordinary, which was a sort of menu for the day and usually very cheaply priced. For those who lost money on the Westwood there was the chance of winning bets at a cockfight for that brutal sport was still popular and may have given the *Cock and Bottle* at Beckside its name. The more civilized attended the assemblies in Norwood and on alternate nights the theatre in Lairgate where special performances were held for them.

Comedy by Candlelight

MUSLIN DRESSES DRIFTED THROUGH the portico and gentlemen in pantaloons laughed and talked cheerfully outside the white brick building, on the corner of Captain Lane and Lairgate, which was Beverley's theatre. It was a bright evening in May, June or July; it had to be because there were no performances in the other months.

Mr Samuel Butler's troupe of actors were in Beverley for the season so the theatre came to life. It was occasionally used for other purposes but never in Race Week when visitors who came to the course on the Westwood, looked for other entertainment in the evening. A special performance would be put on at the theatre which held 532 people and was a modern building, only built seven years before the Regency.

Sadly it is not there any longer but has been demolished. Some of the bricks and the pillars from its entrance were incorporated in a Victorian pub but when the present author went to photograph them, that building too had been demolished But in 1811 the theatre was new and popular.

A lady, alighting from her sedan chair, would be assisted by her husband who had walked beside the chair. There was only room for one person inside which was just as well because the unfortunate chairmen had to carry it. These walked, one at the front and one at the rear, between shafts rather like horses – especially when their breath clouded the air in winter. A wealthy family might own a sedan chair, although there were public ones for hire. If you owned one, you might keep it in the hall of your house but it took up space and it was better to have a proper sedan chair house outside. Newbegin Bar House had one and we can still see its doors if we walk down Newbegin Lane.

The lady, alighting from her chair at the theatre, would certainly be going to sit in one of the boxes. From there she had an uninterrupted view of the stage which was surmounted by "a neat bust of Shakespeare".

The lights in the theatre continued to burn throughout the performance. This meant you couldn't steal a kiss in the dark because there was no concealing darkness. Candles lit the auditorium. It was only on the stage where lights could be dimmed. There the footlights were whale oil lamps which were adjustable.

Seats in the pit were a little cheaper than boxes and the gallery was cheapest of all.

The first week of June 1812 was Race Week. Sportsmen from other places came into Beverley; the inns did a good trade and visitors noted that their evenings need not be dull. There were to be Assemblies and the prospect of going to the theatre. There they got their money's worth for the programme consisted of three items. There was a tragedy and a comedy and between them came an entertainment which might be a song, a dance or some acrobatics. If you didn't feel inclined to sit through the whole of this marathon, you could go for just part of it.

Theatre-goers knew that Samuel Butler and his company of actors would be performing. Some of the visitors had already seen them at York Theatre Royal; many people in Beverley had watched the arrival of their scenery, costumes and other props as they rumbled up Lairgate. Mrs Butler, Samuel's second wife, and their nine year-old boy had come with the company and were staying in Beverley.

Mr Butler was always welcome not only in Beverley, where he had opened the Lairgate theatre, but in Harrogate, York, Whitby, Ripon and Kendal where he was manager of the theatres. It was possible to do this since they each had their own season and he took his company of travelling actors from one to the other.

The 1812 season in Beverley began well and then came a severe shock.

Suddenly, on the 15th of June, Samuel Butler died. Race-goers, Beverlonians and actors were appalled.

His body was buried in St Mary's Church where we can still see the memorial tablet in the south transept with its Shakespearian quotation: "In memory of Samuel Butler, 'a poor player, that struts and frets his hour upon the stage, and then is heard no more.' Obt 15 June 1812, aet 62."

There would be anxiety among the actors. They had depended upon Samuel Butler for their livelihood. What was to happen to them? Besides, Beverley wanted the theatre in action. At this point, Mrs Butler very bravely undertook to run the company and, seven days after she became

Fashion picture from The Ladies' Monthly Museum.

a widow, they performed *The Heir at Law* and *Malvina*. In mid-July they moved on to Harrogate as Samuel had originally planned.

So the usual playgoers crowded into the theatre, a few older or professional gentleman in wigs, ladies dressed in finery for the occasion and young men ready to ogle any pretty actress or member of the audience through a quizzing-glass.

Gentlemen frequently kept their high-crowned hats on in the theatre and might stand at the back talking. Amongst the ladies sitting stiffly on benches, in the pit, there was likely to be at least one who wore an ostrich feather erect above her chignon. Other folk would need to move their heads so they could see round her to the stage. Even those sitting behind the chandeliers in boxes would move around and talk. It was enough to make an actor forget his words. A couple of gentlemen might discuss the merits of the fillies due to race next day whilst a thespian in Hamlet's clothes trod the boards and pondered whether "To be or not to be."

Gentlemen singing.

VII

Sets and Circles

RACE-GOERS WERE NOT the only people to use the Assembly Rooms, although the building was opened specially for them on the Wednesday and Friday evenings of Race Week. Throughout the winter months the Assembly Rooms were used regularly by affluent patrons who had bought shares in the lovely building which had been designed by York's famous architect, John Carr. The older people could remember it being built in 1763. Young ladies in simple Grecian style silk dresses matched the style of the Rooms. Mr Carr had chosen the Greek fashion for his design and embellished the building accordingly with a stone pediment.

When one entered the foyer there were doors to right and left. On the right was a large tea room whilst the left door led to a card room where gentlemen and older ladies repaired to play whilst the younger ones, watched by fond mothers, took part in country dances in the ball-room. This was a regal-looking room of elegant proportions (50x27ft), the walls ornamented with two niches and six Ionic pilasters quite reminiscent of a Greek temple.

Unfortunately we cannot see the long room where couples danced to the top of a set or whirled in star shapes to the music of players who were ensconced in a gallery above the entrance lobby. The Assembly Rooms, then on the West side of Norwood House, have since been demolished.

In 1813 another demolition took place. The old Assembly Rooms in Tiger Lane had been redundant since Mr Carr's beautiful building had been erected in Norwood. They were pulled down in the Regency.

It was quite a status symbol to attend the Assembly Rooms. Only those who could afford the £25 shares had a right to be there. Moreover the Greek building was never sullied by vulgar activities for the trustees refused to allow the rooms to be used for anything other than assemblies.

It was with excited anticipation that the patrons arrived. Some came in sedan chairs, some in carriages. All were beautifully dressed and their

Evening Dresses 1811.

Norwood House. The Assembly Rooms were on its left.

coiffures were soon highlighted by the brilliance of candles reflected in seven glass chandeliers.

The music from the gallery was lively and the dancers got quite out of breath. Many a mama's glance tried to follow her daughter through the twists and turns of the dance. Who was that young man ogling her as she set to the right? What were his prospects?

The violinist and the cellist on the balcony would have a better overall view than Mama. From this vantage point one could see the long columns, revolving stars and circles which formed patterns. It is, however, unlikely that any of the musicians had time to observe the figures of the dance; they were too busy providing its music which sometimes involved swift bow work for some of these maggots included skipping as well as decorous sidesteps. A "maggot" was an idea and most dances were someone's invention and so became known as Mr So-and-So's Maggot.

Fortunately not all the gentlemen sought the card room. The younger ones flirted and danced through most of the evening. If you saw a pretty girl pass you as she and her partner progressed between the two ranks to the top of the set, you could get someone to tell you her name and ask her for a dance yourself. In polite circles partners were introduced to each other before they danced together. It was risky to dance with a girl more than once because the gossips sitting against the wall would soon be pairing you off for life.

When the Assembly was over the chairmen came to collect the ladies, fresh air fanned flushed cheeks and Beverley's gentry went home to bed.

Cash from the Hatter and a Coat for Samuel

BENT NEARLY DOUBLE IN the after part of the ship, tipped out of a hammock that curled round you like a peapod or running up the ratlines when the ship heaved beneath you; these were everyday experiences for a sailor. But what could he do if he lost his sight?

George Tottill was a blind sailor. He and his family tramped through Beverley in 1815; we don't know if he had lost his sight in battle against the French. All we know is that they gave George two shillings to help him on his way. "They" were the Overseers of the Poor.

As there was no National Insurance or state pension, the local area had to provide for its own poor. The money came from the Poor Rate, which was levied on householders, and it was dispensed by the Overseers. They usually paid a shilling a week to the poverty-stricken, provided these poor souls actually lived in the parish; if they didn't, they were sent to the last parish in which they had been settled. "Casual Relief" might be given to someone passing through the town. No one wanted them to stay because, if they did, the Poor Rate would go up.

As it was, it also had to provide for the Workhouse, a building in Minster Moorgate, which housed those so destitute that the shilling a week was not enough to provide for their needs because they had nothing else. They could not even afford to bury their dead so a pauper's funeral was arranged. In May 1815 the Overseers paid Joseph Thwaites nine shillings "for a coffin for Greenberry's child," and 4/6d for burial fees when the small coffin was committed to the earth.

The Overseers had to keep an account book in which they recorded all their outgoings and the income received from the Poor Rate and other sources.

One other source was paternity payments. Thomas Smithers, the hatter, made regular payments for the child to which Sarah Garnett had given birth. He was far from the only one.

Naturally the Workhouse was a constant source of expense. Messrs Middleton and Dyson provided the coal and were paid £11.16s in July 1815. Abraham Hirst was paid for whitewashing the building; he supplied it with goods every week particularly shoes which he both made and mended. Sometimes shoemakers themselves needed help; that same month John Carr was given five shillings and he was a shoemaker. He came from Bridlington but he had a right to be supported by Beverley because he had served his apprenticeship there.

A widow in Hunmanby received 3/6d a week for herself and three children because her deceased husband had been a servant of Mr Artley of Beverley.

Both servitude and apprenticeship conferred the right of "Settlement" which really meant that you were considered an inhabitant of the parish and so eligible for "Parish Relief" if you fell on hard times even if you were living elsewhere.

The Overseers frequently paid the midwife for her services. She was Jane Stephenson and she got five shillings for attending the pregnant Ann Wilson. Sometimes the money was recouped. When Maria Everingham gave birth the expense of the midwife was repaid by "John Todd the Reputed Father." No one knew about DNA.

The fathers were not always Beverley men so the money might come some distance, if it was paid at all. Thomas Chaffer lived in Sowerby; he was expected to pay half-a-crown a week to support his offspring whose mother was Ann Dean. By December 1815 Thomas was thirteen weeks in arrears, then he managed to send £1.12s.6d by Mr Walker's coachman.

Not that the Overseers always collected all the money due. In 1816 there was a meeting of the inhabitants of the Parish of St Mary's, held in the vestry room. When the accounts were produced for the previous financial year, they were not passed because the Overseers had not collected all the Poor Rate. Disapproval was entered in the Minute Book: "Resolved that it is the opinion of this meeting that the present Overseers ought to make up their accounts without furthur delay that their successors in office may proceed in the execution of this duty."

It *was* a duty; you did not choose to be an Overseer. As in other places, responsible members of the community were expected to spend a year as Overseer. They were chosen by the Vestry Meeting and approved by the Justice of the Peace. The Vestry Meeting was not an ecclesiastical body; it simply met in the church vestry and got its name from its venue.

The Guardian had responsibility for carrying out the instructions of the Vestry Meeting. He was John Colver and did his work so well that his annual salary was increased from five pounds to ten pounds.

A new account book was begun in May 1815 and one of its first entries was three shillings to buy a coat for Samuel Rowland "now in jail." His wife was given Casual Relief amounting to £1 which was much more than paupers usually received but hers was not a weekly payment like theirs. Casual Relief was what we might call a "one-off" payment.

The Vestry could ask for the needs of particular destitute people to be met. In the account book we are informed, by someone who had trouble with spelling, that 1/9d was spent for "Jackson's Child a Pair Shoes as ordid at the Meeting". Then 3/9d was disbursed so that John Jackson's infant might also have "frocks and hatt." At the end of October Christopher Tindall was paid "for cloathes as ordered at the meeting 12s". His breeches had already been purchased and were itemised together with postage on a letter from Hull at 6s.4d.

Sometimes it was not necessary to buy the clothes required. In the July of 1817 "Mason's boy" just needed to regain his jacket and shirt, which were at the pawnbroker's. They were redeemed for him at a cost of 5/8d.

In December, to protect her from the cold winter nights, John Peck's wife received a sheet and blanket which cost fourteen shillings.

In 1818 a couple of pairs of shoes were bought for John Harper's children; they cost 7 shillings but George Holgate's ankle boots cost more than ten shillings and he also received 4s.6d for a spade, probably to enable him to find work.

Some people only needed help now and again, like one wife who received occasional relief and whose needs were laconically summed up in one phrase: "husband in jail."

A victim of cold weather was poor Mrs Brownrigg who required embrocation for her knees and was "now in the workhouse." Presumably an arthritic victim of poverty, she could no longer support herself by any means.

No one would want to go in the Workhouse, although it had not yet become the fearsome building of Victoria's reign. Nevertheless one became an inmate living according to the dictates of the Guardian and the constraints of the Poor Law.

It is a relief to discover that the expenses for December 19th to 26th in 1819 included Christmas Dinner, the total spent was six pounds and elevenpence halfpenny.

Various Beverley traders supplied goods to the Workhouse. Mrs White was paid for lamp oil. This was made from Arctic whales and was used to provide lighting for the building in Minster Moorgate. Mr Dyson, from the firm of Middleton and Dyson, provided fuel, or "coals" as Regency people would say. It was Robert Stephenson who supplied such domestic necessities as sweeping brushes, linen sheets, pillowcases and bolstercases, too, for bolsters were commonly used. Two washing tubs came from Joshua Thwaites and cost sixteen shillings.. Dalton, the bricklayer, sent in a bill for 18/9d which was paid in January 1817. Several members of the Dalton family were bricklayers.

One might suppose that men who had withstood the rattle of musketry and the thunder of cannonades in defence of their country would be well treated afterwards. Sadly, many fell on hard times when the war ended and jobs were hard to get. More than once the Overseers of Beverley gave relief to men passing through the town. In January 1817 two shillings was paid to "William Johnson, a soldier and his wife and two children." In March there was ten shillings for "two sailors casual paupers." On another occasion (October 1815) a soldier's wife and child, on their way to Cottingham, were given a shilling.

The accounts had to be checked and accepted regularly and the auditor was usually called the "Visitor". Robert Rigby frequently signed then in this capacity but he was only a visitor in name as he lived, worked and worshipped in Beverley. He was a popular clergyman and we shall learn more about him in another chapter.

The Good, the Guilty and the Gallows

REGISTER SQUARE GOT ITS name because it housed the depository of Wills and Deeds. The Guildhall dominated the Square in gracious splendour and was the venue for the town's Justices of the Peace who gathered in the Magistrates Room and sat in elegant chairs which had been made by Beverley's great craftsman, William Thompson. Besides licensing inns, keeping an eye on the brewers and the Overseer of the Poor, they made sure that enough men were enrolled in the militia and undertook many tasks for which there was no remuneration. Only "gentlemen" of independent means could afford to spend so much time in the public service without a salary – but only gentlemen were thought suitable for such responsibilities.

Chief of these responsibilities was the maintenance of law and order in the town.

The Guildhall contained a Court Room and a Jury Room and there the local magistrates dispensed justice for the good people of Beverley and, more importantly, those who were not so good. They acquitted, fined or imprisoned as they deemed necessary but capital charges were referred to the Assizes in York.

Most of the indictments were for stealing or assault. The worst form of assault and battery was when the victim was described as so badly treated "that his life was greatly despaired of." This phrase was often used and seems to have equated with the modern offence of GBH or Grievous Bodily Harm.

In 1811 John Wainman, a constable going about his lawful duties, was at the receiving end of such an offence. The perpetrator was the innkeeper, William Richardson. He was found not guilty of using "force and arms" but guilty of beating the unfortunate Mr Wainman. The magistrates fined William Richardson ten pounds, a considerable sum then. Perhaps the justices thought that fines should be in proportion to the offender's ability to pay them for when George Walker, the butcher, used "force and arms" against Thomas Siddall so that "his life was greatly despaired of", the magistrates fined the guilty man one pound.

Some people did not learn from their experiences. John Busby, a blacksmith, was brought before the Michaelmas Meeting of magistrates in 1811 on account of beating Martha Seconby but he was not prosecuted. Two years later the blacksmith was in front of the JPs again. This time he was found guilty of beating and wounding Mary Judson. For this he was "To be imprisoned in the Town's gaol two calender months and held to hard labour."

Thefts were variously punished. When John Bates, a linen draper, stole a tea caddy, he had the assistance of a local cordwainer, John Sidebottom, and this was a felony which often landed a man in York prison. The tea caddy was worth tenpence.

Margaret Brown, whose husband William was a corporal in the 69th Regiment of Foot, stole a muslin gown, a blue and yellow cotton gown and a black silk cloak from Ann Plaxton in January 1814. The total value was tenpence and Margaret was imprisoned for three months.

If the thieves were apprentices, the crime was considered particularly bad. Henry Hardy and John Jones were still apprenticed, the first to William Cook a cordwainer and the second to John Wilcox, another cordwainer, when they stole "with force and arms" a joint of veal and a joint of pork (each worth a penny). They also took four glass decanters, some wine and the glasses to put it in, plus bread, butter and cheese. John Arden was their victim and they landed in the town gaol for six months with hard labour and a whipping.

Although theft and assault were the most common charges, the magistrates sometimes had to deal with more unusual crimes. In 1811 Samuel Burnett was brought before Beverley's justices of the peace. He had previously lived in Louth and Beverley's JPs were appalled at what he had done. Robert Norris, their clerk, inscribed the book of indictments in his beautiful handwriting with the full account of the magistrates' opinions of Samuel Burnett. They described him as "a person of a most wicked, lewd, lascivious, depraved and abandoned mind and disposition and wholly lost to all sense of decency, chastity and morality."

Whatever had he done? He was responsible for publishing a booklet which included a couple of illustrations which were "obscene, filthy, indecent and impure." That was not all. The booklet directed gentlemen to a place where , it said, they might find "mares and fillies" to suit them and these were obviously not equines.

Samuel Burnett was imprisoned for a month in the town gaol but it was felt that his conviction ought to be a lesson to all that no one should seek to lead young men astray. So he was condemned to a very old punishment – standing in the pillory for one hour. This was a terrible punishment if a crowd turned violent and threw stones at the pilloried individual. However, some mobs were more humane and the pillory was used far less often than in the past.

As Beverley was the East Riding's county town, it was the venue for the county magistrates but they did not share the Guildhall which belonged to the town of Beverley. The Sessions House was the venue for Justices who dealt with the roads and bridges, beggars and poachers of the East Riding.

In 1814 the architect, Mr Watson of York, probably heaved a sigh of relief because the work on the Sessions House and the House of Correction behind it was complete and the magistrates were satisfied – so satisfied that, when they met in April, they gave Mr Watson one hundred guineas "for his great skill and attention in planning and superin-

The Sessions House.

tending the building." He had been fortunate in the builder who carried out his designs, Mr Bennison. A contemporary writer described the complex of court and gaol and governor's house: "The *tout ensemble*, when viewed at a distance, has the appearance of a noble mansion with its domestic offices." It is not likely that any of the prisoners would have described it like that but they would have been only too glad to view it "at a distance."

Not everyone who walked up the steps of the pillared portico was guilty. Some were the generous friends of men on bail; they would lose their money if they did not bring the accused to court on the stipulated date.

The Sessions House is still there for us to see beside the present police station in the New Walk which was wide and rural-looking in Regency days. But the Sessions House has an awesome appearance and its great pillars dwarf humanity. It can't have helped the accused to see the manacles carved under the pediment. Was it significant that the figure of Justice on top of the building did not have a blindfold? Traditionally the statue, which represents impartiality, is depicted blindfolded but Beverley's Justice could see.

If the magistrates decided that an offence was a capital one, the defendant would be sent under escort to the Assizes at York where he would stand in the elegant court room with its glass dome and Corinthian pilasters. There was something intimidating about a room whose only light came from a glass dome. You could not see outside; the rest of the world could not see you for there were no windows. Even the carved lions looked fierce.

The accused probably wondered what chance he had from a jury composed, like the magistrates, entirely of "gentlemen" which meant property owners. They would not have experienced hardship and might be very unsympathetic.

Yet feelings of acute apprehension could even afflict jurors. No doubt they kept assuring themselves that they were not the accused but the sight of the judge's chair dominating the court room was a reminder of the sentences which had been passed on men indicted for capital crimes – death sentences. The sensitive juror would hope that he would not be in the position of declaring anyone guilty of such an offence. Unfortunately the chances were quite high for over 200 crimes carried the penalty of hanging.

Statue of Justice, Beverley.   *Statue of Justice, York.*

At some time prosecuting counsel would put on his wig, hoist his gown higher on his shoulders and what would happen then?

In 1814 counsel prosecuted James Forbes who had been committed to York by Jonas Brown and John Gilby, two of the East Riding magistrates on charges of murder and theft. Two men swore on oath that James Forbes had used a pistol to shoot John Taylor, wounding him severely before stealing the banknotes and silver coins which Mr Taylor was carrying. This was highway robbery which became more serious when John Taylor later died. The future looked black for James Forbes. Indeed, if the defence did not do a good job, Mr Forbes might have no future at all. But the jury were not convinced of his guilt and so he was discharged.

In the summer of 1815, whilst men were recovering from their wounds at Waterloo, came the drama of the two Johns – Hoggard and Hodgson.

John Hoggard was brought to the Sessions House charged with having killed a sheep and stolen the carcass which was worth twenty shillings. The sheep belonged to John Hodgson and he swore on oath that the young man (Hoggard was 23) had slain and pinched it. The Justice of the

41

Peace, Mr J Robinson Foulis, was convinced and sent John Hoggard to York to await trial.

The modern complaint, that our prisons are overfull, is not new. Georgian county prisons were unhealthily overflowing with the wicked, the pathetic and those awaiting a verdict(which might be Not Guilty). Sometimes local magistrates felt that no more felons could be accommodated and that Gaol Fever – a kind of typhus – would threaten the community. If the Assizes were still some weeks away, a special Assize for Gaol Delivery would be held. Along came two judges to try offences, freeing the innocent and dispatching the guilty to Australia, other prisons and the gallows. An Assize for Gaol Delivery was held at the Castle at York on Saturday 8th July in 1815 and the judges, Sir John Bayley and Sir Richard Richards, came to York.

John Hoggard would be led from his stuffy, smelly, over-inhabited cell to the Law Courts which were at right angles to the prison, and topped with their own figure of Justice. John eventually took his place in the dock which faced the bewigged judge across the court room. He knew only too well that the penalty for sheep-stealing was death. The jury of men, who were accustomed to eat plenty of meat, listened to the

The Court House, Beverley.

prosecution's evidence and John Hoggard had to wait tensely in the dock for their verdict. He was found "Guilty of feloniously killing one wether sheep, with a felonious intent to steal the carcass thereof."

Then the judge put on the black hat known as the Cap of Judgement and pronounced: "...thou shalt hang by the neck until the body be dead..."

It was common for a judge, at the end of the Assizes, to reprieve some of those condemned to death but none of them knew if he would do so or, if he did so, which ones he would reprieve. Perhaps some law-enforcers believed that, "It would do him good" for a felon to face his execution. The late Dr Johnson had said that: "Hanging concentrates the mind." No doubt it also tortured the minds of the condemned man's wife and children.

John Hoggard's mental torment lasted until the end of the Assizes when he was reprieved. In the printed list of verdicts and sentences his guilt is recorded with the word "reprieved". Some hand has written at the side, "Twelve months at Beverley." It is a little difficult now to read the faded ink but it seems that John's execution was commuted to a year in Beverley prison.

Joseph Coltman was a cultured academic and very willing to share his knowledge and love of it with disadvantaged youngsters. Years later when he died, someone wrote: "...he never seemed so happily employed as when he was instructing young men and endeavouring to embue (sic) their minds with that sort of learning of which they had been denied the possession, through narrow circumstances, or a neglected education. He was in truth a father to the fatherless..."

When people did not know where to turn for help, they often turned to Mr Coltman. It was said that no one ever left him without being charmed by his kindness and good sense.

This genial soul grew in corpulence as he grew older and attracted much interest when he began to ride a Hobby-horse, the Regency fore-runner of a bicycle. It wasn't so easy to ride because it had no pedals and so the rider had to provide his own propulsion by "walking" with his feet whilst he sat astride the iron bar. Of course, sailing downhill was exhila-rating. No feet needed then.

Beverley does not seem to have been afflicted with anyone like Jane Austen's Mr Collins. Far from it; besides Joseph Coltman, they had the Revs John Gilby and Robert Rigby.

John Gilby was a prime mover in setting up the East Riding District Society for Promoting the Education of the Poor according to the Principles of the Established Church. Besides his initial donation of ten guineas, Mr Gilby subscribed two guineas a year to it. He worked so hard for this cause that the committee passed a resolution on 11th June 1812: "That the thanks of this Meeting be given to the REV JOHN GILBY, for the zeal he has manifested, and the great pains he has taken in pro-moting the object of this Meeting."

Robert Rigby was vicar of St Mary's throughout the Regency. His congregation did not sit in the present pews. They used galleries which faced each other across the nave. From these they could admire the bon-nets of the ladies opposite, the carved Tudor bosses on the wooden ceil-ing and the Rev Robert Rigby in the three-decker pulpit.

Mr Rigby acquired an extra task in 1811, because William Tesseyman died that year. Five years previously Mr Tesseyman had set aside ten guineas for the benefit of the poor. The interest was to accrue until his death and from then onwards the income was to be used each Christmas to buy bread for 6 poor men and 6 poor women who were regular church atten-ders. By 1811 the capital had become £12.12s and Robert Rigby had to buy sixpenny loaves with the interest and give them to twelve selected and impoverished folk.

In 1812 Mr Rigby spoke at a meeting called to consider starting a local Bible Society and evidently he spoke convincingly because the meeting carried all his proposals. Beverley Corporation subscribed twenty guineas and "several other respectable sums were contributed," said the newspaper.

Robert Rigby served with Joseph Coltman and John Gilby on the committee which had set up schools for poor children in Beverley. Many jobs seem to have been entrusted to him including auditing the accounts of the Overseer of the Poor. At the Vestry Meeting, which had oversight of the provision of rates to help the poor, he was, as we say nowadays, The Chair.

XI

Graffiti and Grumbles

THERE WERE MANY PEOPLE in Regency England who had to sign their name with a cross because they could not write. A literate person would then write beside it: "John Jones, his mark," or other appropriate words. There was no state education so it wasn't a sign of stupidity but poverty which forced a man to put a cross on his wedding lines.

So John Gilby and the other reverend gentlemen who sat on the committee to raise money for schools in the Beverley area were doing a necessary job. They met with others on June 11th 1812 to start the project. The newspaper said it was a "respectable meeting" which really meant that some well-known people were there. These included Thomas Grimston, Thomas Duesbury and Richard Bethell who became chairman. They appointed Joseph Coltman as secretary and decided that they would establish a boys' school and a girls' school. All over the country these schools were being started so they were called National Schools.

Not surprisingly John Lockwood became treasurer. Not much happened in Beverley without reference to Mr Lockwood, a local solicitor who lived in Lairgate and knew how things should be done.

Local people made contributions to this National School and Beverley's was started in a room in Minster Moorgate. Costs had to be kept as low as possible so they used a method tried out by the Rev Andrew Bell, a missionary in Madras. It certainly was an economical system; briefly, it meant that the teacher taught a group of older children who then separated and each went to a different part of the large schoolroom to pass on what they had just learnt to another group of pupils. Called the Monitorial System, this cheap way of teaching cost only five shillings a year per child.

Beverley had some other schools as well as the new National Schools.

There was a very old grammar school for boys at the south-west corner of Minster Yard. The building dated from Stuart times but had no house for the teacher. This caused problems. Sometimes people living in St

Love and Learning.

John's Lane might hear the shatter of breaking glass, a yell of triumph or smothered giggles followed by the pad, pad, pad of running feet. It was Those Boys again. Daylight revealed another broken window in the lovely medieval Minster.

Then there were the graffiti and not just once. Grey heads were shaken and shocked voices bemoaned the decline in morals and behaviour; things had not been like this when they were young. No teacher would have allowed it but nowadays no teacher could see what the lads were up to. There wasn't a schoolmaster in sight. Something ought to be done.

In 1814 something was done: the school was pulled down. After the ancient building was demolished, the pupils found themselves in a new grammar school in Keldgate under the watchful eye of the teacher.

The schoolmaster was given a large house fronting Keldgate. A past pupil, driving his gig down the Street, or a present pupil scurrying past, could not ignore the imposing home of their pedagogue. Weathered by two centuries, it is less obtrusive today.

The new grammar school was opened in 1816 next door to the head-master's house. It may be that the architect felt that an educational institution ought to look old and stately because the new school consisted of a large room in a Gothic design. Perhaps he was merely following one of the Regency's fashions – an attempt to imitate medieval buildings. Those who read Lord Byron or Sir Walter Scott caught the love of castles and monasteries from their writings. At any rate the new school managed to look old. It also managed to contain plenty of boys, being a room fifty feet long and twenty-five wide. And just to make sure everything was under control, "The headmaster's desk was at one end and the assistant master's was at the other." There was a porch at the front and a library above it containing 700 volumes. Probably of more interest to the boys was the Fives Court made in the large playground.

But there were no books available at Graves's Schools and pupils had to provide their own. This school was financed with money bequeathed for the education of poor children by the will of the Rev James Graves so it was called Graves's Schools. The plural was due to the girls and boys being separated. There could be no "goings-on" in Graves's Schools. Mr Cass taught the boys in a big room which was close to the Fish Shambles. Simultaneously his wife taught the girls in a room in Wilkinson's Yard. Mr Graves had left £2400 in 5% stock for the upkeep of the school but it was necessary for the children to pay a shilling each quarter.

Highgate leading to the Minster.

Schoolmaster's house, Keldgate.

In 1814 the trustees decided to admit more children and therefore bought the building in Register Square which had been a theatre before one was opened in Lairgate. A couple of new teachers replaced Mr and Mrs Cass. William Wilkins and his wife were appointed and Mrs Wilkins was expected to spend part of each day teaching the girls needlework. This was probably intended to enable them to earn a living as seamstresses and lady's maids.

Academic work was not considered suitable for females whether poor or rich; there were no places for them at University. It was thought worthwhile teaching them to read, write and add up. That would be necessary for a housewife but a young lady would be better employed making a neat sampler to practice her stitches whilst her brother was expected to read the speeches of Cicero in latin. Some of the gentlemen who frequented the races would be capable of quoting latin even if they were more interested in horses.

Like many towns, Beverley had a Blue Coat School which catered for poor children and was supported by various donations and legacies from people who had left money to Beverley Corporation for the running of this school.

Not that all the bequests were quite so munificent as they seemed. The Trustees found that Sir Griffith Boynton's annual sum had ceased as it was recorded that "...as...Sir G Boynton's affairs appear to have been in a state of great embarrassment at the time of his death it seems to be wholly lost to the charity."

Fortunately there was enough from other benefactors to rent a house in Highgate which had a yard for a play area and a useful piece of garden. They were able to accommodate eight boys, whom they fed and clothed, and to pay the teacher an annual salary of £14.

The boys were taught reading, writing and arithmetic. On winter days, when darkness came early, their schoolroom was warmed by a fire and the coal was paid for out of the trust funds. On Sundays the schoolmaster took them up Highgate into the Minster for the service.

When a boy was old enough to leave school, the Blue Coat Trustees paid the necessary sum to get him an apprenticeship. He would then learn a trade, probably living in his employer's family home, and hoping to become a journeyman – in other words a fully qualified workman able to earn his own living.

There were, of course, some schools for children whose parents could afford to pay fees. However, some of these were run by one person in their own home. These are sometimes called Dame Schools and the Dame did not always have much knowledge to impart. In all, Beverley had fifteen schools but the sons of the gentry would go away to boarding schools.

Sedan Chair House, Newbegin.

XII

Windmills on the Westwood

THE SMELL OF BAKING BREAD was familiar to Regency noses. Many houses and cottages had a bread oven built into a corner. If the cook used a copy of *A New System of Domestic Cookery Formed upon Principles of Economy And Adapted to the Use of Private Families by a Lady*, she would keep new flour four or five weeks before she used it to bake. She probably sent a boy up to the Westwood to buy the flour directly from one of the windmills there. If she really was working on Principles of Economy, the boy was most likely sent to the Union Mill to get it.

The Union Mill got its name because it belonged to a society of people who had invested money in the building and were able to get their flour cheaper there and to receive dividend from the profits made by the mill. For the Union Mill bought wheat, ground it into large quantities of flour and sold them. Although the site belonged to Beverley Corporation, it had been leased for 99 years by the trustees of the mill, Thomas Duesbury, John Lockwood and John Tuke. Today we can still see part of the Union Mill; it has lost some height and been incorporated into the golf clubhouse.

The Union Mill was not alone on the Westwood. Of the five windmills, one belonged to Joseph Baitson, who lived in Wednesday Market. His windmill still dominates the skyline. Today it is black but it was once white and filled with the musty smell of harvest.

When a harvest mouse could perch on an ear of wheat, when the great bay shire horse pulled a wagon up the lane and when Joseph Baitson, standing on his wooden stage and leaning back against the tower, could see golden fields and a blue mist on the horizon, he knew the windmill would soon be busy.

Mr Baitson probably had a flat thumb, a bit spadelike at the end. Most millers had that; it came from rubbing the grain between finger and thumb. We don't know if Joseph Baitson had a nickname but many millers were called Dusty. One only had to look inside the windmill to understand

Union Mill.

Baitson's Mill.

55

why. Flour and chaff blew around when a gusty nor'-easter sent draughts through the tower.

On a sunny day the great sweeps cast rotating shadows on the ground. You could hear the clacking and rumbling of the machinery as the great stones ground the corn and every mill seemed to have its own distinctive sounds.

Hither Mill was another tower mill and would look very artistic when its sails were set like the St Andrew cross. But the real reason for leaving the sweeps in that position was not aesthetic; it was done so that all four sails bore the same amount of stress. That is how they rested through the night and in the morning the miller set them like St George's cross before the day's work began.

When one of the Fishwicks died all the five mills on the Westwood would have their sails stopped at the sign of St George, as the usual mark of respect on the death of a miller. The Fishwick family owned a post mill on the east of the open space near to Butt Close so it was called Fishwick's Mill. It stood on an artificial mound enabling it to benefit from the vagaries of the wind.

For grinding, the sails needed to be on the same side of the mill as the wind. This is the reason for the fantail, a device like a miniature wind-mill fixed to the mill so that when the wind changed direction, the little fantail spun fast in the new direction and turned the mill's cap into the wind. On the tower mills the fantail was fixed to the cap.

However, Fishwick's Mill was an old windmill made of wood and created round a central post. When the sails needed to face a new direc-tion, Mr Fishwick had to use a long pole to turn the whole mill into the wind.

Far Mill had once been a post mill but it had been replaced by a tower mill in 1803 as had Hither mill thirty years earlier. Fishwick's was the last post mill on the Westwood and a lovely old lady she was with her weath-ered boards. All windmills were thought to be feminine and when a miller spoke of "she", he was not speaking of his wife but his mill.

XIII

To War with Wellington

THE SIMMONS FAMILY WERE living in St Mary's Parish in Beverley when the Regency began. They were a large family and Mr Simmons had difficulty making ends meet but he no longer needed to support his eldest son, George, who had been in the army for two years and managed to send some money home to help the family.

George was in Portugal where the British Army was deployed to defend the Portuguese and drive the French out of the Peninsula. George did not wear the scarlet tunic which made most British soldiers easy targets; he was in the crack regiment (the 95th) which wore green jackets. They needed this camouflage for they often acted as snipers. Unlike the rest of the army which used a smooth-bore musket nicknamed Brown Bess, the 95th had been issued with rifles and trained to be good marksmen.

When a man went to war his family lost touch with him for months. A young wife would not describe parting as "such sweet pleasure" for she could not follow her husband's progress. Not for her a brief televisual glimpse of his regiment in the battle area. She might imagine him tossing in the Bay of Biscay in a transport ship with all sails tied to the shrouds but she had no means of hearing from him until months and months had passed. Probably, as she rocked a wooden cradle with her foot and looked at the small face inside it she wondered if her baby's father was still alive.

In 1811 George Simmons was involved in house-to-house fighting as the 95th regiment pursued the French to the mountains. The army had no tents so at night he and his comrades used to fix blankets over sticks to give themselves some shelter. Some men had to cobble blankets together to make a pair of trousers for their regulation grey trousers had worn out.

Beverlonians might imagine a victorious well-fed regiment in scarlet jackets marching triumphantly. They could not see the reality of faded jackets and men with empty stomachs because the bread supply had run out. On one occasion they had meat to eat but nothing with it and even

Soldiers in 1814.

58

Duke of Wellington.

that was luxury for on occasion they subsisted on beans, grabbed from a field, or acorns in the mountains.

George, who was promoted to lieutenant, got ague when the army besieged Ciudad Rodrigo. It was bitterly cold and his whole body shook. He played his part in capturing the place and after attacking by night, he got a good breakfast – bacon and eggs with wine. He didn't know the danger he was in whilst he ate his tasty food. Some barrels of gunpowder were below the ramparts but as he was chewing ham above them he couldn't see the danger. But some hours later he heard that powder blow up and saw that his "breakfast room" had disappeared.

Joseph Simmons left Beverley that year and joined the army. Soon he, too, was in the Peninsula. Then, in 1813, a third of the Simmons sons became a soldier but he went into the 34th Regiment and wore the red coat typical of the British Army. So he became one of the "Lobsters" or "Rosbifs" as the French called them. His real name was not much better; he was called Maud after his aunt.

George was already a seasoned campaigner and had been wounded twice in his country's service when Maud arrived so he felt a sense of responsibility for his younger brother. As Maud was in another regiment, he could not protect him much but he gave him useful advice. Joseph and George, on the other hand, actually fought together at the Battle of Vittoria. Maud was also in that important victory but his regiment was in a different part of the battlefield. He sustained a slight wound but George was already experienced at tending wounded men. After the crossing of the Nivelle he nursed his badly wounded commanding officer and was given a gold watch as a thank-you.

The three brothers spent Christmas 1813 together. They had been in Spain for some time and heard that their parents had left Beverley for Anlaby. But we cannot leave these brave young men in the Pyrennees even if their parents were no longer Beverlonians.

The climb over the mountains was excruciating. We all experience sore fingertips in cold weather but the soldiers sometimes experienced that painful sensation all over their bodies. Frost formed on trousers and some men, literally stiff with cold, actually froze to the ground and had to be wrenched to their feet in the morning.

Wellington's army crossed over the border and faced the French on their own territory in 1814. The Simmons "lads" were invaders. A musket ball broke George's knee. Maud had been given responsibility for billeting so he found a sympathetic landlady for George and was able to visit him frequently.

The three Simmonses were in Bordeaux in June 1814 where the 95th were to embark for England and the 34th for Ireland. They could not know that they would never all be together again but all partings in wartime are disturbing. Maud had another nine years before he would die on service in India. George had yet to fight at Waterloo.

In that campaign he received admiration again from Sir Andrew Barnard, the colonel who had given him the gold watch. On June 15th part of Wellington's army was stationed at Quatre Bras, the crossroads on the Charleroi *chaussee* where they tried to prevent the French advancing towards Brussels. One of the men was terribly wounded; George and another went stealthily towards a French picket and snatched the man to safety. Sir Andrew called it: "A glorious act."

After a saturating deluge with dramatic lightning and thunder, the allies took up position on the 18th before the village of Waterloo. In that defining battle the 95th were positioned at another crossroads. When the farmhouse, obliquely opposite to them, was taken by the enemy, French soldiers brought up a couple of guns and pointed them at the 95th. They loaded them with merciless grapeshot – the name given to bundles of

The colours and uniform of the old East York.

musket balls designed to spray into the British ranks and kill as many men as possible.

George was hit by a musket ball which broke two ribs, tore his liver and lodged near his spine. The successful end of the battle was a time of intense pain for him.

The news of the victory at Waterloo reached Beverley by stage-coach and newspapers. The ecstatic townspeople felt heartfelt relief and thrills of pride. They learnt of the charge of the Scots Greys but they didn't wander over the battlefield which was covered in dead and dying horses and men.

They couldn't hear the cries of wounded men or the weak voice of one soldier boy who asked his friends to tell his parents he loved them but never to let his mother know about the pain he suffered as he died.

Contemporary prints showed a fat jolly John Bull waving Napoleon away from the shores of Britain, confident he couldn't land. Our men would prevent him. But John Bull had no idea at what a cost. In the Peninsula one Beverley officer was killed by a cannon-ball and from the same family General Ford Bowes was killed leading his men at the Battle of Salamanca.

Just suppose that Napoleon had landed, what would have happened? The people of Beverley would have been protected by the militia. At least, that was the plan.

The militia was made up of men who continued to live at home and do their daily jobs. Each place had to provide a given number and they went for training for a fortnight when they learnt to march and fire a musket. The East Riding Militia of 3,400 men were divided into four groups and one of these was based in Beverley. They would be called up for their practice fortnight by the Lord Lieutenant's orders but these orders were conveyed by the Clerk to the Lieutenancy who was, unsurprisingly, John Lockwood. Any man who had not been on militia exercises previously had to arrive a week earlier for preliminary training.

They made a splendid sight in scarlet coats with muskets at the ready. They marched and countermarched watched appreciatively by those who thought what a wonderful display of bravery this was.

After the fortnight they went home to their farms and shops and labouring jobs.

XIV

Market Stalls and Humber Keels

THERE WAS MUCH BUSTLE IN Saturday Market. Farmers' wives brought large baskets of produce and sat beside them awaiting purchasers; the more practical among them had brought three-legged stools which stood firmer on the cobbles than four-legged ones.

They never traded in Wednesday Market because, despite its name, it was not a market place.

Mellow brick houses overlooked the Saturday Market. The *King's Head* was an inn with a particularly good view. It did good trade and had stabling for sixty horses when its landlord, Israel Marshall, died and it was sold in 1811. All the furniture and the "brewing utensils" were in the sale, too. In the second half of the Regency Mr Witty was the landlord. We can still see the *King's Head* but it has been altered. It was a three-storey building with a balcony and was the venue for members of the Union Mill Society.

Inns were useful places, not merely for food, drink, beds and horses, but also because they had public rooms where committees of various kinds could meet. An inn with a balcony was specially useful and many towns had one. The *Beverley Arms* (alias the *Blue Bell*) had a balcony which was used by the candidate at a General Election to show himself to the crowd.

Those, who lived in houses beside Saturday Market, did not need to look out of the window to know that it was market day; the sounds conveyed that message. Hooves clopped across cobbles, voices shouted wares, men carrying large loads called to others to get out of the way. Rumbling wheels, barking dogs and shrieking children completed the cacophony. There was also much snorting and squealing from the north end of the market place where the pigs were sold and Sow Hill perpetuates the memory of them. Any trader who sold a pig had to pay a farthing toll to the corporation unless he was a Freeman of Beverley. There was a list of tolls levied on farmers and others who sold their wares in the market.

The Market Place, Beverley.

Corn chandlers repaired to the Corn Exchange, a brick edifice, and the name Cornhill reminds us of the wheat grown on the Wolds, ground at one of the windmills and sold in Beverley. An even larger area was set aside for the sale of butter.

Thirsty men called at the house (now named *The Push*) where there was home-brewed beer for sale. Prosperous farmers went into the *King's Head*, the *Beverley Arms* or the *Tiger*.

The eighteenth century market cross presided over the crowded scene.

Four times a year a vast mooing surrounded the town because they held quarterly markets devoted to cattle . No one could be in any doubt of what was happening as the drovers brought the beasts to the market place.

Then there were the fairs, also once a quarter; large sums of money changed hands. Many cattle were sold at the fairs,too, and traders from Hull came to buy chickens and eggs for resale in that town. With so many transactions taking place, the Beverley bankers offered facilities at fair times.

Some prosperous landowners would have money to invest. Other farmers might want to try some of the new ideas promoted in the Annals of Agriculture but hadn't enough money. Such a farmer would need a bank to lend him the capital outlay.

The "Big Five" did not exist but wealthy men could set up their own banks where they took money on deposit and paid interest to the depositor whilst also lending at interest to others.

The East Riding Bank was in Lairgate and was run by Messrs. Bower, Duesbury, Hall and Thompson. It had been established by Sir Christopher Sykes and had branches in Hull and Malton. Not surprisingly the influential John Lockwood was a partner in this bank.

At North Bar Within there was another bank, owned by Machell, Pease and Liddell, which was called simply The Beverley Bank.

It shows how prosperous Beverley was that it needed these banks. In 1818 a Savings Bank was started in Hengate. After only a year nearly eleven thousand pounds had been invested there and that was a vast sum in Regency days.

A bank could be a very cosy place on a winter afternoon with a fire glowing in the hearth whilst the clerk dipped his pen in the large inkstand and entered the transactions into the ledger with his beautiful calligraphy.

Private banks were allowed to print their own notes as long as they had security for them. Both the Beverley Bank and the East Riding Bank issued their own £5 notes. This paper money was used for trading in the locality because people there knew that the paper really was worth what was printed on it.

Beverlonians felt that their money was as safe in local banknotes as it would be in Bank of England notes – or it ought to be.

In 1813 thirty-seven year-old John Smith was in Hull Gaol because he had been charged with stealing from Richard Coates a black leather pocket-book with five guinea notes of the East Riding Bank of Beverley and some notes issued by different banks in Hull. On the 6th of March his prison door opened and he was taken over the Wolds to York Assizes where the judge sitting on the case was Mr Gros. The jury found John Smith Not Guilty and the judge discharged him.

Although Beverley banknotes were accepted in East Yorkshire, people in other parts of the country had not heard of the Beverley Bank or the East Riding Bank so they would be very reluctant to accept their notes. This could be a problem when someone from Beverley visited London.

However, the East Riding Bank had an arrangement with Messrs Curries, Raikes and Co in London whereby that bank would honour their notes and serve their customers when in the capital. The Beverley Bank had the same arrangement with Sir Richard Carr, Glynn and Co, another London bank. These metropolitan banks were known as "agents" and because of them Beverley people did not find themselves short of cash when staying in the capital.

Getting off the stage-coach in London was a daunting experience for anyone who had never ventured far from Beverley previously. The noise, the size and the stench of parts of London could be overwhelming. To make matters worse, some artful Londoners waited to see country folk alight from the stage in the hope of cheating them.

One young man from Beverley arrived in London in March 1812. As he crossed over Blackfriars Bridge, a couple of Cockneys pretended to pick up a leather box and immediately accosted the young man. Look what they'd found! A diamond cross and here was the bill for it – over two thousand pounds! As he'd seen them pick it up, would he like them to share the proceeds with him? He said he would and accompanied them to an inn near Fleet Market. But they never got an opportunity to sell the jewel.

The King's Head.

The Beverley Arms.

Beckside.

The honest young Beverlonian was too wise for them. He looked round the tap room and called out to the company there that the two men were sharpers. The two quickly disappeared leaving the so-called diamond cross with him. Its real value was eighteen shillings.

Beverlonians learnt to be honest traders and to know the true value of saleable goods. Beckside was the scene of much coming and going of merchandise. The Beck had been made navigable a decade before the Regency so goods imported at Hull could be transferred to smaller craft and sent by water to Beverley.

Beckside was a place of tranquil reflections until stirred by a shivering breeze. At other times it was a scene of commercial activity. Keels were much wider in the beam than longboats so many imported goods were trans-shipped to them in Hull and glided upstream to Beverley

Large square sails approached up the waterway as a Humber keel brought a load of hides to the tanners of Beverley who needed even more than they could obtain from the carcasses of East Riding cattle. There was great demand for leather goods: breeches, boots, shoes, saddles, bridles and even buckets were among the items made of leather and the tanneries needed to supplement their hides from Russia. The Beckside was really a little inland port connected by the River Hull and the Humber to the docks where Baltic cargoes were unloaded at Hull. Although Beverley was a market town and the centre for an agricultural area, it was also a venue for overseas trade.

William Cook junior, a boot and shoemaker, worked in Beckside where he could collect imported hides.

Skins from smaller animals such as sheep and goats were also imported so Beverley's tanneries could keep working profitably.

Sometimes coal was unloaded so the Beckside was a good place for coal merchants and seven had premises there: Christopher Eden, John Hodgson senior, John and Thomas Lee, James Thompson and the firm of Webster and Hodgson.

The town charged tolls on merchandise brought for sale. It was a busy job collecting the tolls so the corporation sold the right to collect the money and allowed the collector to make what he could with a table of agreed toll prices; for example, on every dozen calf skins one penny, for every quarter of bark (used in tanning) one halfpenny. Webster and Hodgson, the merchants, had paid four or five hundred pounds to the corporation for the right to collect the tolls. It shows how many loads of goods passed through the Beck that Messrs Webster and Hodgson could make in excess of £400 or £500 by collecting such modest amounts as one shilling for every dozen chairs, one penny every quarter of oatmeal and for every hide a farthing.

Beckside was one of the busiest parts of Beverley. Naturally it provided opportunities for lots of people. George Smith was one of them; a joiner, housebuilder and wheelwright, this specialist in woodwork had his premises in Beckside. A heavily laden waggon, creaking its way to the river bank, needed attention and George Smith was the man for the job. Working at his wheel-pit, he would hammer spokes into a stock; the banging of his sledgehammer would add to the many noises beside the Beck.

William Cooper's smithy was at Beckside and here patient draught horses could receive new shoes. Probably Roger Dawson brought him trade because Mr Dawson was a cartman. William Cooper would make other items besides horseshoes; braces and brackets and innumerable iron implements made to the customer's requirements kept his forge busy.

Beverley's affluence was reflected in the loads of corn sent down the Beck for sale. Most of the corn factors also dealt in coal. Colliers brought coal from Newcastle to Hull and then it travelled by water to Beverley and waggons could take it still furthur inland.

As Beckside was an industrial and commercial centre, the dull rumbling of wheels mingled with the metallic ringing of the blacksmith's hammer on his anvil and the tumbling of a load of coal.

It was the sort of work which gave a man a dry throat. Fortunately help was at hand; five hostelries stood at the Beckside. There was the *Black Horse* which changed its name to *The Anchor* during the Regency. The *Buck Inn* now has a new frontage but it seems to have been typical of a Vale of York house, having two front rooms with a kitchen behind them. An archway gave access to the back yard. The present *Foster's Arms* occupies the site of the old *Cock and Bottle* of Regency days and even incorporates one of the original entrances; looking at the building now we can hardly imagine the old *Cock and Bottle* where John Dove brewed fine beer. A woman was in charge of the *Golden Fleece*; Sarah Elstob was the landlady of this old building beside the turnpike.

William Lowther was innkeeper at *The Sloop*, an inn well-named beside a navigable river. Occasionally the mast of a sloop would tower above the water; she was fore-and-aft rigged, unlike the broad square-rigged keel so often seen there. Mr Lowther's sloop was a simple, mid-18th century building; upstairs at the back there is still a Yorkshire light.

So much activity crowded into Beckside, even including distilling, bleaching, sewing and making straw hats. Thomas Southwick was a shopkeeper who could supply fabrics and make men's coats.

Beverley's shopkeepers could supply most needs. The chemist, Mr Turner, sold many remedies and even stocked Nelson's Restorative Tooth Powder which was used "Not only by their Majesties but by the principal Nobility and Gentry in the kingdom."

Not that Beverley's shopkeepers were always spreading happiness and good-feeling. In 1811 one of the druggists was incensed with a shoemaker. It so happened that the shoemaker was a sergeant in the Volunteers, a smartly-uniformed group of gentlemen who swore to fight the French if they landed. To his fury, the druggist called him a coward. Him! A coward! To show he wasn't, he at once challenged the druggist to a duel. Preparations were made for the encounter and the sergeant arrived to prove his valour. He never needed to put it to the test because his adversary, who disapproved of duels, didn't turn up.

The Volunteers made a splendid show in their uniforms but it was a little unfortunate that local people were apt to mispronounce the word "corps". When the corps of Beverley Volunteers were on parade, a number of women were overheard saying that they had "Seen how well the corpses look."

XV

The Burgesses of Beverley

IN ONE PARTICULAR MATTER Beverley was very fortunate; at General Elections it could send two members to Parliament. Not only was this twice as many as any constituency today, it was 100% more than many big towns in Regency England. Neither Manchester nor Birmingham could send a representative to Westminster. Beverley was much smaller than either of them but it had been a town far longer. When constituencies were being established, some places simply did not exist but Beverley had been there since long before the first Parliament.

Of course, in those pre-Suffragette days no women had a vote but neither did many men. The rules differed from place to place. In Beverley the Freemen could vote although some of them did not live there. A Freeman was allowed to trade in the town so many of the electors were shopkeepers. In all there were about two thousand men who had the franchise in Beverley.

Voting could be a risky business because your vote was recorded in a book and the poll lists were published. Anyway, you could be heard naming your favoured candidate on the platform where the votes were cast.

In 1812 a General Election was called suddenly for a most unforeseen reason. The Prime Minister was murdered. He was Mr Spencer Perceval, father of twelve children, and was walking through the lobby of the House of Commons when a demented man with a grievance raised a pistol and shot Mr Perceval through the heart.

At the time John Lockwood was Mayor of Beverley and Mr Wharton was one of Beverley's MPs, having been elected in 1807 along with R W Howard Vyse Esq. Mr Wharton was well-known on the Beverley Race Course where he was one of the stewards. As soon as it became obvious that a General Election would be called, he sat in his residence at Skelton Castle and wrote a letter to the Beverley voters to be published in the newspapers. He reminded them that he had represented them for 22 years and added: "I beg to assure you that, should you again confer on me the high distinction to which I aspire, my best and unremitting shall, as

72

North Bar Without.

heretofore, be used to promote and secure the Honour and Interests of my Country, and of my Constituents.

    I am,

        Gentlemen,

    With sincere gratitude and respect

        Your obliged and faithful servant,

           John Wharton"

His hopes were fulfilled. When the voters of Beverley climbed onto the voting platform, many of them spoke his name to the clerk who made the record of votes.

The gratified Mr Wharton wrote another letter to the York newspapers thanking them for their confidence and assuring them: "Believe me, I never solicited it from motives of ambition, or the hope of deriving therefrom any Personal Advantage, but from an ardent wish to render service to my country; And you, Gentlemen, by delegating to me for the FIFTH TIME this sacred trust have furnished me with an additional stimulus to use increasing diligence and exertion in the faithful discharge of my Parliamentary Duty, and you may rest assured, I shall ever act under its influence."

So wrote a satisfied candidate. The other one was Charles Forbes. In 1818 Mr Wharton was again re-elected and on that occasion the other MP was R C Burton, Esq.

North Aisle, St Mary's Church.

XVI

Parish Pews

MOLESCROFT WAS A VERY SMALL village with about thirty inhabitants so it did not possess a church. St Mary's on the north end of Beverley was well placed for the villagers to use so it might be expected that they would worship there. Not so. An accident of history had placed them in the parish of St John and every Sunday the faithful walked through the Bar, past St Mary's and right through the town to pray in the Minster. Young ladies approached St Mary's from nearby, their thin-soled shoes no protection from the knobbly cobbles. Sunday bonnets nodded as they greeted young people from Molescroft on their way to the Minster.

The hollow ring of hooves on stone announced the arrival of a couple of the gentry who might come in a curricle which waited outside, the groom's tall boots highly polished for Sunday and the horses with gleaming bay coats.

Inside childish fingers played with a prayer book and wandering eyes sought the angels on the Tudor ceiling. In summer bright light shone through the clerestory windows; in winter flickering candles cast shadows.

Pews on the north side faced southwards across the aisle. It was easy to see who was sitting opposite and to avoid or seek their gaze whilst Mr Rigby declaimed his sermon from the three-decker pulpit, typical of Georgian times. On Sundays worshippers always sat in the nave where galleries had been added. We cannot see the Georgian pews, which were replaced with the present ones in Victoria's reign, but we know they were high-sided and people sitting in them would be able to look up at the wooden ceiling made in Tudor times which we can still see today.

During the weekdays people had daily glimpses of St Mary's Church. It did one good to look at the tower of the old church where generations had found peace and hope. Many of the streets had been laid out at angles which enabled folk to see the tower. This deliberate planning meant that the shopper coming out of a bow-windowed shop saw St Mary's tower

St Mary's seen down the street.

immediately on stepping outside. However, they did not see flying buttresses by the south transept; those have been added since Regency days.

Meanwhile at the Minster, the slim long-skirted young ladies, conscious of their bonnets and their friends, sat in the cool nave with older ladies – just as self-conscious in their Sunday best.

Devout eyes looked to the aspiring lines of the east window, with its medieval and clear glass reflecting the light, to feel, as Wordsworth had so recently written that:

"Sense sublime of something far more deeply interfused
Whose dwelling is the light of setting suns..."

Beverley Minster.

Bibliography

Ashton, John: *The Dawn of the Nineteenth Century in England*

Ayling, Stanley: *George the Third*

Baines: *Yorkshire (1823)*

Brooke, John: *King George III*

Cary, John: *Roads (1819)*

Capman, Ben and Maeve: *Beverley in Old Picture Postcards*

Chester, Don: *The Fighting Simmonses of Beverley*

Crowther, Jan: *Beverley in Victorian Times*

Cruikshank, Dan: *A Guide to the Georgian Buildings of Britain and Ireland*

Frost, Phyl: *Molescroft, Beverley's Northern Neighbour*

Gibson, Paul: *A Toast to the Town. (A History of Beverley's Inns)*

Gillett, Edward: *The Humber Region at War 1793–1815*

Gregory, Roy: *East Yorkshire Windmills*

Gregory, Roy: *The Other Beverley*

Hadfield, Charles: *British Canals*

Hall, Ivan and Elizabeth: *Historic Beverley*

Hoskin, Rev David: *A Guide to St Mary's Church, Beverley*

Jackson, Gordon: *Hull in the Eighteenth Century*

Kincaid, Sir John: *Adventures in the Rifle Brigade*

Lyth, John: *Glimpses of Early Methodism in York (1885)*

McLynn, Frank: *Crime and Punishment in Eighteenth Century England*

Mitford, Mary Russell: *Our Village (1824-1832)*

Moody, Berna: *Doorways into Beverley's Past*

Neave, David and Susan: *East Riding Chapels and Meeting Houses*

Neave, David and Susan: *The Diary of a Yorkshire Gentleman. John Courtney of Beverley 1759-68*

Doorcase.

Fanlight.

79

Norfolk, RWS: Militia, Yeomanry and Volunteer Forces of the East Riding 1689-1908

Paterson, Daniel: *Roads (1784)*

Pinfold, Frank and Higginson, George: *The Inn Places of Beverley*

Poulson, George: *History of Beverley (1829)*

Rosenfeld, Sybil: *The Georgian Theatre of Richmond Yorks and Its Circuit*

Sturt, George: *The Wheelwright's Shop*

Victoria History Of Yorks East Riding

Watson, J Steven: *The Reign of George III*

DOCUMENTARY SOURCES

York Herald 1811-12

Churchwarden's Account Book, St Mary's 1815-19

Minster Churchwarden's Account Book 1815

Overseer of the Poor Accounts Book 1815-16

Quarter Sessions Order Book 1811-17

Calendar of Felons and Gaol Delivery York Castle 1800-19

Indictments from Beverley Quarter Sessions 1811-15

Contemporary Prints

Beverley St Mary's Monumental Inscriptions: David Mount *et al*